Walking by
Faith
and Not by
Sight

(It Pays Off)

Natasha Scott

WESTBOW
PRESS®
A DIVISION OF THOMAS NELSON
& ZONDERVAN

WestBow Press books may be ordered through booksellers or by contacting:

WestBow Press
A Division of Thomas Nelson & Zondervan
1663 Liberty Drive
Bloomington, IN 47403
www.westbowpress.com
844-714-3454

Scripture quotations are taken from the Holy Bible, New Living Translation, copyright ©1996, 2004, 2015 by Tyndale House Foundation. Used by permission of Tyndale House Publishers, Carol Stream, Illinois 60188. All rights reserved.

Scripture quotations taken from The Holy Bible, New International Version® NIV® Copyright © 1973 1978 1984 2011 by Biblica, Inc. TM. Used by permission. All rights reserved worldwide.

ISBN: 978-1-6642-4955-4 (sc)
ISBN: 978-1-6642-4956-1 (hc)
ISBN: 978-1-6642-4954-7 (e)

Library of Congress Control Number: 2021923052

Print information available on the last page.

WestBow Press rev. date: 11/17/2021

Dedication

This book is dedicated to my husband James Andrew Scott, I love that God blessed you as my soul mate, I'm blessed on how we met and how we build a family and a future together. I love the part that you are mines and I am yours whatever ever door God opens for us we would walk through it together. Love you your wife.

Contents

Introduction

"For I know the plans I have for you,"
declares the Lord, "plans to prosper
you and not to harm you, plans to
give you hope and a future."
—Jeremiah 29:11 (NIV)

THIS BOOK IS ABOUT A WOMAN WHO HAD BIG DREAMS IN LIFE TO become a registered nurse. She planned to become successful, independent and wealthy until she got off course, falling into what she thought was love with a man that had no stability, no goal, and no ambition. He was up and down in his religious belief in God, and the only thing he had going for himself was his decent paying job.

He did have his own car, leading her to believe he had a lot of stability and independence in his life.

This man that she thought she was in love with was unhappy about the choices he made in life. They took her on his roller-coaster ride that lasted for two years; within those years she ended up with two children and no marriage. They started not to get along very well, knowing that sex before marriage was wrong in the sight of the Lord.

The ups and downs in their relationship led her, walking by faith and not by sight, on a vacation to North Carolina. On that vacation she was away for a month, and within that time away from her hometown she met someone special whom she fell in love with at first sight, not knowing that the man she fell in love with was a seeker and a believer in the Lord with a high calling on his life. Her trip paid off, since the love of her life is now her husband. They got married in 2004 and have been blessed with six children and with grandchildren. They both are servants of the Lord, saved by God's grace and mercy.

This book is based on real-life events inspired and quoted by the New Living Translation (of the Bible). This book relates a story that can lift your mind, heal your heart, and give you strength, hope, and courage. I hope it helps you realize that faith is not about what we see; it's about what we don't see. It's about trusting in God, believing he will give us all that we need to get through life. All quoted scriptures (taken from the NLT, the New Living Translation) are inspired by God.

1

The Day I Went Blind

Now faith is confidence in what we hope for
and assurance about what we do not see.
—Hebrews 11:1 (NIV)

IT ALL BEGAN DECEMBER 31, 2000, NEW YEAR'S EVE, WHEN I was sitting in my apartment hoping for a change in my life, I was home with my two boys in a town known for shootings and killings. That bothered me, but at the time I had no choice. I didn't believe in laying up on anyone with the responsibilities that followed me; the streets would say no one would want me with baggage.

I was a single mother with two boys, one and two years of age. The babies' father was in and out of our lives. He tried to be that family man, but he wasn't qualified. When it got too hot in the kitchen, he ran; truly indeed the kitchen had been hot for some time now.

It was 11:00 p.m. The pressure was on me to make a change for the better. My New Year's resolution was to get my life back; this time I would be getting it back with two children I fell deeply in love with.

When midnight struck, with a, "Happy New Year 2001!" my resolution was written out on a piece of paper, and I hung it up on the refrigerator with satisfaction. Like everyone on New Year's, you want to celebrate your new beginnings, starting the new year off with a toast. At the time I was not a wine or champagne drinker; I drank beer. I had too much, and it took me off course from what my first plan was when I was sober-minded.

In my drunken rage I took the paper off the refrigerator and ripped it up. I felt as if I'd brought in the new year like a failure. Instead, I felt hopeless, overwhelmed beyond imagination. I cried almost every night praying that morning would reveal a better hope for me and my two boys. One thing about me: I was proactive, but not active enough to make wise decisions.

Tax Season

It's better to take refuge in the
Lord than to trust in people.
—Psalm 118:8

I was home with my two boys getting them ready for bed. After they were asleep was when I meditated and prayed to God, who I truly believed in. Growing up as a child, I was brought to church and taught about Jesus, but I never took the time to get to know who he really was except when I was in trouble or depressed. I can remember getting intimate with the Lord in conversation, but then I started feeling silly talking to myself, not realizing I was talking to the almighty God. The deeper the conversation grew, the sillier I began to feel.

Then I heard an aggressive knock at the door. My children's father was standing there, drunk. I should've known that when you do good, evil is always present, but because of my vulnerability, I let him in. Although he came in talking sweetly, I should've known that alcohol gives you liquid courage to convey your deceptions. Again, he caught me at a vulnerable time.

He started to talk, and I began to listen. Soon he was telling me about our future and what we could have together. I was all for his conversation because he was saying all the right things, but his actions had never stood for what he said. Still, I listened that night, giving him the benefit of the doubt. He even shed some tears as he apologized for not being with me and the children. He promised he would become the father that he should be, and a husband that I hoped and prayed for.

He needed one thing from me to accomplish all of this: the children's Social Security numbers so he could claim them on his taxes. He said, "When the money comes, we can build a better future, get married and live like a family." I believed him and I gave him their numbers.

The next day we went to H&R Block, and he did his taxes. He would be getting back eight thousand dollars. I started telling Jesus, "Thank you, thank you for answering my prayers." The tax office told us we should receive a check in a few weeks.

My kids' father always had a little money on him, so after we left the tax place, we bought lunch to take to my house. On the way home, he was talking about all the good things I wanted him to say. He also said, "Let's stop by a car dealership and test drive our first family car." I was so happy that the new year had finally started to pick up great value. At the car lot I picked out a green 2000 Kia Sportage, and he said he would get it when the tax money came.

My kids' father worked full-time, so money was good at times. He stayed with the kids and me for a few weeks waiting for the check to come; it was the best few weeks with him in a long time. He went next door to call H&R Block and came back to tell me that the check was ready for pickup; we both were happy. He told me to stay home and get the kids ready for the day, and he would go pick up the check and come back.

He never came back. I was heated beyond heated. He had persuaded me that the change for us would be real, but it turned out to be the untruth all over again. I was back to how I was feeling on New Year's Eve—hopeless and overwhelmed beyond imagination, but this time with added anger and hate.

I had to do something quick to make me feel good again, at this point I'm eager for revenge. All types of evil thoughts were playing out in my mind, but at the same time a part of me didn't want to act because of God's Love I had within me. Two wrongs don't make things right and knowing that I left it in God's hands. The best hand's you can leave any situation whether it's good or evil.

2

Leave It in God's Hands

*My hands have made both heaven
and earth; they and everything in
them are mine. I will bless those
who have humble and contrite
hearts, who tremble at my word.*
— Isaiah 66:2

FAITH UNFOLDS BY LEAVING ALL THINGS IN GOD'S HANDS AND by beholding his hand in all things.

March and April were struggling months for me. My happiness came from seeing my two boys happy. We had a routine every morning: wake up, eat breakfast, take a walk to the park, and stay all day until evening. Then we would walk over to my aunt's house or my mother's house for dinner. They both lived within walking distance.

My children loved our daily outings. If they were smiling, I was smiling, but my smile was like the tears of a clown. I felt so down, discouraged, hopeless, lost, useless, and embarrassed; then the tears would start to come. As my kids were running and chasing one another in the park, I would be talking to God, saying, "Why, why, why did I put my faith in this guy and not trust in God? It seems like when I met this guy, my life turned for the worse before that I had it going on. I was independent, happy, wealthy, and content, working at the hospital as a CNA studying to be a registered nurse. Then I got deceived and knocked off course by one of Jesus's fallen angels appearing to be light, but I found darkness instead. Every time I start getting intimate with the Lord, that's when someone will show up, and I'll stop talking with God."

At this moment a family of four came into the park, a mother, father, and two children, and here I was at the park as a single babies' momma, miserable, and you have to understand: the last thing I wanted to see was somebody in possession of the very thing that I was crying out to

God for. I told the boys we were leaving the park and they began to cry. "We don't want to go back home yet; we want to play more," so I let them. They didn't realize that I didn't like to be around people in this state of mind; they did not understand my depression. I kept saying to myself, "I'm going to leave this situation in God's hands." But it's easier said than done.

Finally we left the park, and I was on my way to my aunt's house. She lived in an interesting building, a building where you would find people like me, miserable. She lived on the sixth floor. The boys loved going there because she allowed them to do what they wanted. My aunt was as sweet as sugar, and I loved her. I would sit over there and pour my heart out to her about these kids' father on how he didn't want any part of them. She would then say something like "That's him missing out on the good times when they're young and growing up and need that father figure in their life. When they grow up, they're not going to want anything do with him." But she always told me not to talk disrespectfully about him to them but teach them to respect him. When my aunt saw that I was a little down, she would always find a way to uplift my spirit by quoting a scripture or telling me to leave it in God's hands—"he will work it out." Then she would say, "Let's order Chinese food, and get what you want."

Leaving her house that evening I felt great. Approaching my house, I would always say to the Lord, "Thank you for watching over me and the boys as we walk the dangerous streets." Then, after reaching my apartment, I got my kids ready for bed, and then I poured a relaxing beer into a glass. That one glass turned into a few more, and soon I was drunk and passed out until the next morning.

The next morning I woke up and looked at the clock. It was after eight in the morning, and a strange feeling came over me. I didn't realize it then, but knowing the Lord the way I know him now, it was his Spirit warning me that something was wrong. I jumped out my bed and saw that my kids were missing. I began to call them in rage, yelling their names. I looked at the front door and saw it was cracked; my kids had left the house. I found them across the street at the park.

The first thing I did was acknowledge the Lord by saying, "Thank you, Jesus!" He kept them safe from seen and unseen harm and danger. The second thing I did was give both of them a spanking, letting them know how dangerous it was to leave the house without a parent, and I soon realized I was the one that needed one also for getting drunk and neglecting my responsibilities. My kids knew our routine, and I had messed it up. I apologized to them, hugging them and saying, "I will make this up to you guys."

At this point I said, *"Lord, help me!* I'm beginning to feel like I'm an alcoholic." I said, "Lord, I'm leaving my situation in your hands." Sincerely I began to say, "If I only had money, I would buy clothes and a charter bus ticket to go down south for a month. I'll look for a place out there to get away from this depressed situation that I am in and start all over with my life."

I went on a fast, not knowing anything about fasting or its power, how real it was. I did remember that when I was a kid, my grandmother would always say, "If you want God to move, turn your plate down for him."

So I did it for two days. In those two days I was continually pleading my case with the almighty Lord, saying, "Lord, I know you can do all things but fail, and right now I am desperately in need of a breakthrough.

3

Breakthrough

For his anger lasts only a moment,
but his favor lasts a lifetime! Weeping
may last through the night, but
joy comes with the morning.
— Psalm 30:5

AFTER TWO DAYS OF FASTING, I WOKE UP WITH A LOT OF strength, feeling very accomplished. I was starting to find that joy that I once lost. I was feeling like that independent CNA studying to be a registered nurse. Even though having children changed my life from that dream, God was working on another one within me.

As I was preparing for the day, I started hearing a voice. I started to think I was losing my mind, not knowing at that moment that God was letting me know everything was going to be all right. It seemed as if God was really on me that morning. I felt like a press and a strong presence. That strange feeling drove me out the house more quickly than usual, but running outside didn't solve the problem. That same feeling followed me outside and throughout the day. I then realized that no matter where we go, God is a spirit, and no matter what we do when he wants our attention, he is always present.

The kids and I did our usual park play, and I sat on the swing talking with the Lord. Afternoon came, and I was led to go home instead of visiting as usual at my aunt's house. Once again God's Spirit was being the mighty shepherd now, guiding me to where I needed to go at that time.

The Mailbox

To everything there is a season, and a
time to every purpose under the heaven.
—Ecclesiastes 3:1

As I was coming home from the park, the mailman was just leaving. The kids and I walked over, and I opened the mailbox. A bunch of mail came out like it was Christmas. I noticed there were two envelopes from the state, and the rest of the mail was junk. I was concerned about those state letters, so I rushed back in the house and tore the envelope open like a savage and there was a check in there for two thousand dollars from back-owed child support.

Boy, was I crying for joy, saying God had made a way of escape for me and my kids to travel down south. I was so excited that the Lord had answered my prayers. I told my boys, "Let's get to my aunt's house before she receives the phone call from her daughter." My cousin would call her mom at a certain time each day, and sometimes I was there when she called. I wanted to make sure I was there that evening so I could ask her if I could come stay with her for the month of May.

When I arrived at my aunt's house she saw that I was full of excitement and asked, "What's all the grinning about?" I told her that the Lord was really showing himself in my life. "I came into some money, the breakthrough that I was praying for, and it will pay for my trip down south." She was overjoyed at how quickly God was moving on my behalf. She also was excited that I was going away for so long. Seeing how God was moving so quickly in my life, she was eager to see what he had planned for me next, and so was I.

My cousin called, and I asked her if I could come to her house for the month of May, and she said absolutely. Then she thought I was playing because we joked together like that to the point that we didn't believe each other, but this time it was a different situation. God had this planned, and now I was walking by faith. It was Wednesday, and I went summer shopping for me and the boys. When my mom got off work, she took me to the Greyhound bus station. I bought a round-trip ticket leaving that Friday evening and returning in June. My mom was surprised by my decision. She was shocked I was taking off for so long with two baby boys.

My aunt was with us and couldn't believe it either, but God was dealing with me with my faith and trust in him, showing me then that it is better to walk by faith and not by sight.

4

Walk by Faith and Not by Sight

*Now we see things imperfectly, like puzzling
reflections in a mirror, but then we will see
everything with perfect clarity. All that I
know now is partial and incomplete, but
then I will know everything completely,
just as God now knows me completely.*
—1 Corinthians 13:12

I WAS HOME PACKING MY BAGS GETTING READY FOR MY TRIP.
Friday evening was a day away, and I couldn't wait to
board the bus. I talked to my children that night on how
we were going away to have fun with family in another
state. They were happy, just to see their new clothes going

into the suitcase and me making sandwiches for our ride. I took a long bath that night, and as I was meditating, I remember reading a verse in 1 Peter 1:7: "These trials will show that your faith is genuine. It is being tested as fire tests and purifies gold. So, when your faith is far more precious than mere gold. So, when your faith remains strong through many trials, it will bring you much praise and glory and honor on the day when Jesus Christ is revealed to the whole world." I smiled for a long time letting that scripture feed my spirit.

Soon I was out of tub and dressing for bed, and I heard an aggressive knock at the door. It flashed me back to New Year's—that same aggressive knock that sounded too familiar. I paced back and forth, debating whether I should open it, and my spirit was telling me no. At that moment my flesh was warring. I did remember on my fast reading the scripture in Galatians 5:17: "The sinful nature wants to do evil, which is just the opposite of what the Spirit wants. And the Spirit gives us desires that are the opposite of what the sinful nature desires. These two forces are constantly fighting each other, so you are not free to carry out your good intentions."

The knock turned to kicks at the door. I was afraid my kids' father was going to wake them. Then he went to their window and was trying to open it. I couldn't call the cops or anyone for help because I didn't have a house phone, and cell phones were not popular at the time. So I began to do the next best thing, and that was calling the name Jesus, praying that he would stop and just go away. "My intentions are on a positive note, and I don't want him near me or my children. He has no clue I'm leaving town in the next twenty-four hours." I did not want him knowing what my plans were. If he knew, he would do all in his power to stop us. Soon he simply did stop and left.

When morning came, my kids and I woke up and ate breakfast, and as I was dressing them, I let them know this was the day for vacation, and everything we did would be for a limited time. We went to the park, and they played while I was swinging and talking with God, letting him know that I was afraid to travel alone with two babies. I let Jesus know that the stories I heard about the New York bus station were scary, and I asked him to please watch over us and make sure we got to the right terminal. That was my fear.

While I was talking with God, I heard a familiar voice approaching us, and it was my kids' father. The kids ran to him and said, "We are going on vacation." I was upset because I didn't want him to know that. (He didn't seem to catch what they said about going on vacation.)

He started asking me questions and arguing with me about last night, on why I didn't open the door. He said I had another man in there, which I did not. He began to act in a very negative way. His behavior was out of control. Someone saw him and called to me that if I needed help, they would call the cops. The cops showed up, and my kids' father took off. The officers could see how disturbed I was, but I deflected all their questions and said I was fine.

I left the park and walked to my aunt's house. I felt safe there for a while because she had a house phone, just in case I needed to call the cops. The phone rang when I arrived, and it was my cousin getting the details of my travel and when I would arrive. Time was running out, so I went home to get fresh for my departure.

My mom and aunt took me to the bus station and sent me off. The boys were happy on the bus. I was sad because this was the first trip away with my boys, leaving my aunt and mom, but happy I was getting away from my kids' father. Four weeks was a long time, but the change was for the better. The better change was that now I was walking by faith and not by sight, and I was beginning to realize that faith isn't always easy, but it will always work out for the best.

5

Change for the Better

Anyone who belongs to Christ has
become a new person. The old life
is gone; a new life has begun!
—2 Corinthians 5:17

ON MAY 1, 2001, I ARRIVED IN NORTH CAROLINA, LEAVING
forty-degree weather and entering eighty-degree weather.
The atmosphere was different, and the air was fresh.
We got off the bus, stripping off our jackets. As we were
waiting for our luggage from the bottom of the bus, my
cousin called my name with a big smile and greeted me
with a hearty hug. That hug was everything; I was so

happy to be with her and her children. We stopped at Hardee's, my first meal in the Carolinas and the first time in a long time I enjoyed what I ate with an appetite. I felt free; I felt happy.

On our way to my cousin's house she gave me a tour of Charlotte. As I looked out the window, I was saying to myself, *I can make this state my home; I can live out here.* She showed me the new apartments they were building and even took me to fill out some applications. I really was digging this city for my home. The first day in a new state, the kids enjoyed the park and the water park. They had a ball to the point of exhaustion. When evening came, I felt exhausted myself, ready to go shower and relax.

My cousin showed me her neighborhood and the community store called Mr. Lees. Mr. Lees was a hang spot. Out front were pay phones where you could make and receive calls. I used that phone to call home to let my mom know I had made it; I also gave her the number to the pay phone and times when she could call me there. My cousin didn't have a house phone, which explained why she called her mom at certain times of the day.

At my cousin's house, she showed me to my bedroom, where I would be residing for the month of my stay. It seemed as if she gave me the biggest room in the house, I guess because I was her favorite cousin. The kids and I showered and went to bed.

The next day I woke up asking God to guide me into making the right choice. Right now, my choice was never to go back to my hometown. I wanted to start looking for a job and day care for my kids, apply for state assistance, and go from there. I always knew that anywhere I lay my head, I could make my home very comfortably. I was told I snap back from any situation quickly.

Here we were in North Carolina, loving it to the fullest with no care in the world. Every day my cousin and I did something with the kids. At the time she had four kids, and my two made six kids. We dealt with all of them together every day with joy.

Weeks went by, and I started feeling like the kids' father was looking for us. He had no idea where we were unless he had contacted my mother. To be honest, I didn't care how he felt. I was glad I left town and hadn't said a word.

Don't get me wrong; I thought we could've made a great couple, but sometimes your thoughts are not the thoughts of the Lord. Sometimes we ask Why this? or Why that? It's simply because God knows what's best for you. The Bible tells us,

> "My thoughts are nothing like your thoughts,"
> says the Lord. "And my ways are far beyond
> anything you could imagine." (Isaiah 55:8)

Indeed, as more weeks went by, I grew lonely in the way of needing a companion. I became so desperate that whenever any guy said hi, I was like, "What's up?" I did meet a guy, but he stood me up. I'm kind of glad he did. It had been months since I was in a relationship. My kids' father was a joke at this point. Right now I was looking for love. When you ask with a sincere heart, you shall receive. I believed the Lord when he said the effective prayer of a righteous person has great power and produces wonderful results.

6

The Effective Prayer

Don't worry about anything; instead,
pray about everything. Tell God what you
need, and thank him for all he has done.
—Philippians 4:6

HERE I WAS IN MY ROOM, WHILE THE KIDS WERE ASLEEP, thanking God for what he had done and for what he was going to do. My intentions while praying were real and heartfelt. I was asking the Lord to send me someone like me, someone who understood me, someone I understood, someone that didn't mind me speaking and praying to God, amen and good night.

I knew lying in bed that praying with wrong motives cannot be effective. I knew I had God's attention. Being in North Carolina gave me hope again. Everyone I came across was very respectful, something I wasn't used to. Still, I always was very watchful and prayerful. My grandmother always said you have to be careful when you see a wolf in sheep's clothing. I saw as an adult what she meant. She also said that a dangerous person pretending to be harmless is an enemy disguised as a friend; that's a wolf in sheep's clothing. For me as a kid my grandmother was full of wisdom; now that I was an adult, I could relate to her wisdom.

The next day I was low on funds. My mother told me if I needed something, I should ask, and she would send it Western Union. So here I was looking for my mom to come through with what I needed, but God had a different plan to supply. What I really needed was to see him move once again.

I went up to Mr. Lees and the pay phones, expecting a phone call from my mom. As I drove up, I saw a man with muscles all painted up smoking a cigar and leaning on the very pay phone I was expecting a call from. God has a sense of humor; he shows up when you least expect it. I was hoping the man would leave, but he didn't. This was a part of my walk I wasn't supposed to see. I was bold enough to ask this guy if the pay phone had rung since he'd been here. He said no and started walking away toward the store. Then he turned back around as if he was being led by faith and not by sight, the very same Spirit of God that led us both to the pay phone at this time. He asked me where I was from. "Are you from New York City?"

I said, "No, Connecticut." Then we started to converse. He was carrying on about how strong my accent was and how much he missed the city slang since he'd been in Charlotte. Then I asked him where he was from, and he said the Bronx.

I asked him what he was doing out here; he said, "Long story." I said I would love to hear it, and we made a date to see each other that night at eight, at Mr. Lees. I forgot all about receiving the phone call from my mom. I rushed back to my cousin's house with butterflies, blushing, feeling good that I finally had a date. I couldn't stop smiling. I asked my cousin if it was cool if he came by, and she was all for it.

> Don't forget to show hospitality to strangers,
> for some who have done this have entertained
> angels without realizing it! (Hebrews 13:2)

This guy that I met up with that evening was like heaven-sent. James was all right in a man, which I was not used to. I had come from the babies' father, who was verbally and physically abusive to this heaven-sent. I was careful with this guy because of what I had been through. A lot was going on in my mind. I wasn't looking for Mr. Right; I was looking for conversation while away from home—nothing serious, with no strings attached.

This guy I met turned out to be someone I didn't expect. There was something different and unique about James. One night with him changed my outlook on love, but I kept telling myself he was just like all other guys; this was too good to be true. But the more I spent time with this guy, I was falling in love with him. Still, I didn't want to show it or say it.

From the day I met him and invited him into my space, he was always reading the Bible. I found that to be strange because he smoked constantly when he read, and I was taught you couldn't serve two masters—either you were for God or Satan. But there was something about this guy, and it didn't matter to me. He had my full attention, respect, and all the rest.

He had a lot of manners and respect. For starters, I must say, he was humble at all times. I wasn't used to that; you could get him mad, and he still maintained his integrity. That was what turned me on to him. I fell in love at first sight. Yes, I did.

The first night James was interested in knowing about me, and of course I told him half of the truth, but he shared the whole truth with me. I was playing games, but he wasn't. The more we talked, the more we were getting to know one another, and then one thing led to another. The night with him was awesome.

The next day I woke up and he was gone. I felt very guilty and convicted, because I knew sex before marriage was wrong in the sight of the Lord. I started to feel as if I was just used for the one night, and that was it. I never knew when he left, and then I started having feelings of being back home, but I kept convincing myself it was just a night that I should forget.

I went on with my day, but it was hard because all I kept thinking about was him: why did he just leave without telling me? The time I did spend with him felt so perfect in the moment. As time went on, I was hoping he'd come back. I was enjoying his company. No sooner than I hoped that he would come back, there was a knock on my cousin's door. It was him asking if I was home. At last it seemed that I had found perfection in a man. I started to realize that it wasn't the perfection in him, because no man is perfect, but he was seeking after the Spirit, striving for perfection, and the light truly attracted me from the darkness.

7

Perfection

*For you know that when your faith is
tested, your endurance has a chance
to grow. So let it grow, for when your
endurance is fully developed, you will be
perfect and complete, needing nothing.*
—James 1:3–4

I WAS BUBBLY WITH EXCITEMENT INSIDE. I DIDN'T KNOW HOW TO
express my feelings outwardly without being buzzed off a
few beers, but God was in control now, teaching me a new
way of life. James offered to go buy some food and spend
more time with me. I was happy about it. We walked

up to the store with the two boys walking in front of us. He reached for my hand to hold, and I felt loved at that moment. As we entered the store, he said to me, "Get what you and the boys want," and I did.

As I was getting food, drinks, chips, and candy, I was saying to myself, *My Lord, I never felt genuinely cared for by a stranger.* This stranger I was starting to get to know well. I had two weeks left in North Carolina with this new love I met, and every second we spent with one another, I was falling deeply in love. He really took care of my boys as if they were his. He played with them and conversed with them, and they were getting comfortable around him and starting to fall in love with him too. Every night my love and I would stay up late talking.

> *As iron sharpens iron, so a*
> *friend sharpens a friend.*
> —Proverbs 27:17

One night James chose to tell me more about himself and how he ended up in North Carolina. So here we were, lights dimmed, enjoying each other's company. My children were fed and fast asleep. We made a pallet on the floor, and he began to tell me that back in the Bronx, his mother had died when he was the age of five, and his grandmother had raised him until he was fourteen. Then one day he came home from school and found her in the hallway of their apartment struggling to breathe; she gasped her last breath in front of him.

He never met his father, who was Dominican and was deported back to Santo Domingo before he was born. He told me that he heard stories from his grandmother that his mother and father were in love, and they went to college together. He believed the cause of his mother's death was that she was depressed behind his father's deportation, and she gave up on all her medications and the will to live. He went on to tell me how he was put in the state's custody for months until his grandmother's close relatives tracked him down, and they took over guardianship.

All I could say after that story was wow. I told him I was sorry for his losses, and he didn't really want to share anymore, so we read the Bible to one another and went off to sleep. He always would leave out before I would awake. The next morning came, and now I was interested in how he ended up in North Carolina. His story that he shared with me was very heartfelt and interesting, to where I wanted to know more about him.

All day I was hoping he'd come back. I shared his story with my cousin, and she felt sorry for him, she started to ask me whether I knew where he lived in town, and I began to wonder whether he had a girl that he lived with and was cheating on her with me, because of how he would leave out early in the morning. That was something to ask him when I saw him again.

I went on with my day, and evening came. It was around five, and the kids and I were outside. I looked up, and he was coming down the street with bags in his hands. He had bought dinner for the whole house. We were excited, especially me; I couldn't stop smiling. Night fell, and I did my usual, getting the boys ready for bed so I could spend time with my love. I couldn't wait to bathe and then chill. Ready for getting to know how he ended up in North Carolina. That had been bugging me all day, and I had a few questions to ask him. Hopefully he could answer them with the truth.

After my bath, I went into the room where he was waiting for me. He had bought us chicken, we ate and conversed. As we were eating, I asked him, where he went in the early morning, and he told me he worked for a temp agency. Then I asked him where he lived and who he lived with, and he said, "I live on the street." He said he had been homeless for a year and six months. I assumed he lived in an actual shelter for men, but he said no, the actual street, on a cardboard box. He went on to tell me the reason why he read the Bible was because he found out that it is more valuable than anything ever created. That was the very reason why he was at peace with his situation.

It was so sad to hear that I actually was teary-eyed. I told him as long as I was here, he could chill with me. After hearing his story, I immediately extended my stay in the Carolinas for an extra two weeks. I was supposed to go back up north next week, but because of him I stayed longer.

Then he shared with me how he ended up in North Carolina. He was in an extensive line of crime that led him to become a millionaire. He said his last line of adventure was robbing big-time drug dealers, but his last robbery went all wrong, and he found himself broke, alone, and homeless. Then he told me that by living out on the street, he found God. Finding God is beautiful, but that story shook me up a great deal. I began to feel strange around him.

He carried a bag that I started to find suspicious. I was in the room with him but nervous at this point, not knowing who I fell in love with. He told me his name was James Scott, but now I didn't believe it. He had no ID to show me; I didn't know his age or his date of birth.

So it seemed I was in love with a gang banger who shot people for money. He stopped talking and started to read the Bible. As usual, I listened to him read and ended up falling asleep. Then I woke up the next day to find him gone, and I was relieved.

I told my cousin the story James had shared with me, and she was nervous. I told her, "If he comes back, don't let him in. We could have our kids around a dangerous man, a man who may be on America's Most Wanted."

My cousin and I were in her living room watching *America's Most Wanted* to see if James's face popped up on the FBI's list. No success, so we took the kids out for a ride and then to the grocery store to pick up dinner. Evening came, and my kids and I ate dinner, and then I sat out on the porch to see if James would show up, but he never did. I went to bed as usual, finding it strange he never came by. At the same time I was relieved after the last horror story he had shared with me.

Following a second night without James, the next day I got up, concerned about him. I asked my cousin if we could go out looking for him. We went to all the shelters in town, every hangout corner we could think of. No James. I was a little sad because I'd fallen in love with him, but at the same time I started to have mixed feelings because of what he was involved in.

Later that evening I did my usual, fed the kids and put them to bed. I went into the living room with my cousin and talked with her for about an hour, letting her know I kind of missed him being with me at night. I missed the Bible studies we shared for the past few weeks. She said maybe he'd left town or gone back to New York. I was up late feeling sad and lonely.

I fell asleep and awoke to a tap on my shoulder, hearing my name called out softly. "Tasha, it's me, James."

I jumped up and asked, with a tremor in my voice, "How did you get in?"

He was puzzled by my response because he felt that there was no problem with him coming back. Of course, he was unaware of the talks my cousin and I had about him, not knowing we'd tried to find out if he was America's Most Wanted. I do remember telling my cousin not to let him in, but she did anyway because of how I felt before I went to bed. I was glad to see him but angry that he'd been gone for a few days with no word about where he was.

He took a shower, and then he explained to me where he'd been. He said he had to straighten out some friends he had been staying on the street with who called themselves the brotherhood. They were upset with him because they didn't know where he was. He told them he'd met someone special and that he believed it could lead to something great. They were happy for him and concerned at the same time because of all the crimes against homeless people, even murder. He also told me he had a two-day job out in another town. I understood because we had no way of contact.

The next day we slept in, which was great. He had no work the next day, so he took my cousin, the kids, and me out to a Chinese buffet. We ate like kings and queens; we had a ball. He took me to where he'd slept the night before we met. There was his backpack, under a bush. I cried; I couldn't believe that this good man lived on the street.

Time was running out for me. I invited him to come up north, and he responded that he would love to, but he wouldn't come right away. He wanted to save money before he came. I had two days left in the Carolinas, and I was sad to leave James behind, but he had me convinced that he would come.

My cousin felt she should take the trip with me to see her mom. I convinced her that she should, but what about James? She said he could stay at her house with her boyfriend until he saved enough money to come up north.

One day left, and I was packing my bags, saying my goodbyes to the man I was in love with. He saw us off as we boarded the charter bus, my cousin and her kids with me and my boys. I felt comfortable in leaving my love behind. I knew that he wouldn't be living on the street, and soon he would be with me up north.

8

My Sight Has Returned

So we don't look at the troubles we can
see now; rather, we fix our gaze on things
that cannot be seen. For the things
we see now will soon be gone, but the
things we cannot see will last forever.
—2 Corinthians 4:18

ARRIVING BACK HOME WAS VERY DIFFICULT. THE JOURNEY HAD
been too quick, and I felt incomplete because the man
I'd fallen in love with, who finally completed me, did not
return with me. I did leave him knowing that he would

soon come when he made enough money working at the temp agency; at least I hoped he would still come.

So here we were, back in Connecticut, our destination— back to reality. My cousin and I took separate cabs from the station because we were going to different locations. Before we departed, we made plans to meet up later that evening. The kids and I received a cab, and it took us back to our apartment. Frowning with disgust, I sighed the whole way home.

When I got there, I unpacked, and within seconds a knock sounded at the door—as if I was being watched entering my apartment. I asked who it was, and my kids' father replied, "It's me. Open the door." When I did, he greeted me with an unpleasant welcome asking me where I'd been and who I was with, along with his kids. Before I could answer, he was tearing off my clothes with great aggression, demanding, "Who is he, who is he?"

Before I could answer him, he took advantage of me disrespectfully. I was screaming, "No! No!, Don't do that, not cool! Not cool!" He didn't care. I began to tell him I was in love with someone who would soon move in with me. He was in such disbelief, he started to get verbally abusive, so loudly that the neighbors heard everything.

I felt so awkward. I called James and told him how I was approached coming back home. I let him know I'd been taken advantage of sexually, and he was upset. I hung up in tears because from the tone of the conversation, the man I love was probably having second thoughts about coming to Connecticut. James did not sound convinced at all that this took place without being consensual.

Still, in that very moment of hearing James's voice, I knew he was the one for me. How we met was special, spiritual, and divine. Our talks, our Bible studies, and our laughs could not be compared to anything I had ever experienced with another man. I cried about what had happened, praying that James would see how I felt, caught in the middle of loving him and disconnecting from my kids' father. However, my new prayer was that the Lord convinced James to walk by faith and not by what he was seeing. I couldn't help but feel as though if he had come north when I left, things would have been different. But only God knows, and he knows best. One thing was for sure: I wanted James to know I shared everything with him, whether it is good or bad.

In the afternoon my children and I were on our way to my aunt's house to meet up with my cousin and her kids. I told my cousin what had happened, and she was speechless. We took the kids to the community park in the area and we began to pray that my situation would get better. As we departed, she went back to her mother's home, and I went back to my apartment. I began to call the name of Jesus until I fell asleep.

When I awoke the next day, my sight had been returned through the love of God and true love that I had begun to experience once again with James. I realized that what had happened to me I could never let happen again. *That was not love, and God is love. Today is a new day, a day that wasn't promised to me or my two boys.* I began to walk with a positive attitude, preparing my home and myself for James.

One afternoon at our set time, I called him at the pay phone where we had met. This particular time we were happy to hear from one another, and I asked him how his stay was at my cousin's house. He began to tell me that his stay wasn't the same since we left. He also said that he'd been saving money, and he was almost ready to purchase his ticket to come to Connecticut. I said I couldn't wait for him to come up.

He asked if I was sure I wanted this; the uncertainty of the situation that took place the last time we spoke between my kids' father and myself was really eating him up. In our talks he also told me that he was tired of in-and-out relationships with women with no dedication and no promise of a future. I was absolutely, positively sure I wanted him to come.

I could still feel his hesitation from his tone of voice because of the sexual situation that took place, which I had never reported to the police the way James wanted. I felt that if I reported it, the authorities would not believe me because of the two kids I'd had with him, but at the same time, looking outside myself through my love's eyes, I could see how he questioned my loyalty.

Weeks went by, and my children's father hadn't been seen or heard from. It figures; that is just like the devil. When the Lord cleans something up, here comes the devil to mess it up and leave it. I remembered the pictures James and I took in North Carolina. I got them developed and started hanging them all around the walls in the house.

I was happy to show my mom and my sister who I fell in love with. I also told them he was coming to visit soon, but never told them that he was actually moving in with me. My mom and sister thought I was moving too fast, bringing a strange man from North Carolina all the way up here. They were right about the fast part, but when God gives you a great feeling about things down on the inside of your spirit, you move.

As the Fourth of July weekend arrived, the countdown began. James would be coming to stay up north in August of 2001. I was so happy.

I recalled the day I went blind and how I walked by faith to North Carolina. While I was there, I met a good man, a God-fearing man, who was soon to come live with me. I felt so good in my spirit and so happy that I started feeling good about myself all over again. The day I woke up and gained sight again to what God was doing in my life, all I could do was thank him!

The kids and I were on the porch getting fresh air. I was blowing bubbles and they were gleefully popping them until their father came walking by. He looked at me and said I looked nice. He asked me who I was all dolled up for. At first, I ignored him. Then I told him how ironic it was that he knew when I was outside or in my house. I asked him if he had a spy on me. He laughed and boldly told me he had been chilling with a female in the same building as me but on the other side. He told me he had been with her for some time now, and she was cool on how he had a baby's mother in the same building.

I wasn't shocked about the female but was kind of stunned at how bold he was to be that close. As he tried to make conversation with me, I gave it straight to him how I was in love with a man I had met in North Carolina, and I let him know he was soon to come up. I also told him that there was nothing between us anymore ever.

I said I would much appreciate if he kept his relationship between him and his boys. I made it known that I wanted him to leave me alone. I also told him he couldn't be popping up the way he had been doing, because that would be disrespectful to my new relationship. I was him getting upset by the minute at my boldness, and he changed the subject to ask if he might use my bathroom. I said. "You know where it is."

He went in to use the bathroom. After a while, I went in to see why it was taking him so long. I found him going through my room, and he took James's pictures off my wall and ripped them up. As he was leaving, he said, "You can have that dude; I'm good." He left, slamming the door so hard that the wall mirror fell and broke.

I was upset. The pictures were irreplaceable. I was in tears, saying to myself, "This is it; I don't want to see him ever again. I can't wait until James comes—I need him right now." The boys were looking afraid. I comforted them by taking them for a walk to my aunt's house to use her phone to call James. He didn't pick up, so I waited at her house for some hours calling that pay phone, but he never answered it.

My cousin was packing to leave the next morning. As she was getting her clothes and children ready, that was my opportunity to let her know how much I appreciated her allowing me and my children into her space for the month of May. I said how God had used her to play a major role in one of the most special events in my life—meeting James. She said anytime I wanted to visit not to hesitate to ask. As I was saying my goodbyes, I let my aunt know I would come by in the morning to use the phone.

I went home and the only thing I kept saying was that I must get a house phone. The next day, I quickly got up, dressed my boys, and was heading to my aunt's house to call James. As I was leaving my apartment, I was approached by a guy offering housing cable in the neighborhood and a telephone line. I thought, *What a coincidence.* I asked how much, and he said forty for each package or an even eighty dollars for both. I could afford to add that to my budget, so I bought the package. He said he would have it connected within the hour with a phone number.

I was so excited, no more leaving the house to use the phone. So within the hour I went both to my aunt's and mother's house to see if any of them had an extra phone or TV that I could borrow temporarily until I got my own. Boy, did the Lord smile on me once again with a blessing—both a TV and a phone. I went home and hooked everything up.

Then I called James until I finally I got through. When he answered hello, for the first time I called him Babe with a voice full of love and excitement. The name *Babe* was so genuine within me, I couldn't believe that it had come out of my mouth, and I grinned.

We both had good news to exchange. He told me he was leaving tonight to come up north and that he would be with me in the morning. In turn, I gave him my new house phone number. My goodness, things were working out great and perfectly in my favor. After hanging up the phone with James I looked in the mirror and told myself, "It just got real."

9

It Just Got Real

*You can pray for anything, and if
you have faith, you will receive it.*
—Matthew 21:22

AFTER I HUNG UP THE PHONE FROM TALKING TO MY BABY, I WAS in disbelief that reality was happening. In the next twelve hours I would be locking lips and hugging with the man I fell in love with a few months ago. Prayer really works when your faith is there.

I couldn't sleep a wink because of my excitement. I told the boys that James was on his way to live with us, but because they were so small, they didn't understand the plan that God was putting together. They smiled, but I don't think they quite got the joy that was taking place in our lives for the better. No more misery from someone I didn't get along with; no more mental or physical abuse. No man could ever add up to the love God had blessed me with.

It was getting late, and I finally fell asleep. Then I woke up to the phone ringing and James's voice saying, "I'm here." I jumped out of the bed as if I'd heard the fire alarm going off. I told him I had overslept and asked him if he didn't mind taking the bus if I gave him detailed instructions.

I felt bad at starting off wrong by not being downtown to meet him. I could imagine how he must have felt. It is one thing to imagine something you want to happen; it is a totally different thing when your imagination becomes real, and believe me when I tell you that reality just got real when I realized he was actually here.

As we hung up the phone, I quickly showered and got dressed to meet him outside my apartment at the bus stop a little ways from my house. I waited, filled with all kinds of anxiety, disbelief, nervousness, and happiness. I was feeling everything because this was a bold move. Older people always say when you're in love you do the most unbelievable things that nobody can understand.

So here came the bus, and tears started rolling. At that moment I realized that the love James had for me was real enough for him to walk by faith and not what he was seeing. At this very moment of the jitters I was feeling, I realized this man must love me too, to come all the way from being homeless, independent, and hardworking, to giving all that up for me, little old insecure me who felt I would never feel confident again. Something about this man gave me a good feeling about faith, who I was, and what I was truly worth.

As the bus approached down the street, I was teary-eyed. When the bus stopped, he walked right off, and I froze. The greeting wasn't the greatest because I was still in disbelief that the man I loved was actually in my face, in the very state where I was brought up. I hugged him tight, but I could've done better with the greeting. Instead, I grew shy. I don't know what came over me, but deep inside I was very, very happy to see him. I hoped I wasn't starting to have mixed feelings, and I hoped he wasn't starting to have mixed feelings too.

10

Mixed Feelings

*The human heart is the most deceitful of
all things, and desperately wicked. Who
really knows how bad it is? But I, the
Lord, search all hearts and examine secret
motives. I give all people their due rewards,
according to what their actions deserve.*
—Jeremiah 17:9-10

QUICKLY MONTHS WENT BY, AND JAMES AND I WERE KICKING IT
good. He ended up finding a job at a temp agency. Life
was good for us—until one day the hot love we had for one
another started turning warm. My kids' father had a lot

to do with the mixed love I started having because of his deceitful ways. He was acting like he wanted his family back but, his intention was to destroy my relationship with James.

James started to feel I was being deceitful with my feelings toward him. I was deceiving myself from the true feelings I had toward the new love I had found, trying to convince myself that the old love I had really wanted his family back together. At times James and I would disagree back and forth with one another about who I wanted to be with, him or my kids' father. The truth was I wanted James, but my kids' father started threatening me on the things he would do if I didn't get him out of my house around his kids. He began to make up untruthful things to assassinate my character as a responsible parent, things that could get the state involved. Soon I feared that he would take action, so one day I made up this lie that I was moving, and I told James he had one day to leave my home, and he did.

One week went by, and I hadn't heard from my kids' father or James. I started feeling like a lowlife because I had allowed my kids' father to tell me to remove the love of my life out of my house or he would call the state. I felt very foolish that the man I fell in love with was gone forever.

All I could do was think about James—how uncertain he felt, his hesitation to come, and his doubts about my loyalty—and how this situation must have confirmed all his feelings.

Two or three weeks went by, and I cried every day, praying that James would call me or come by. But because of the way I'd acted and kicked him out, I knew that was too good to hope for. I started feeling as if I deserved every pain and loneliness at this point of my life.

After four weeks, I was missing James intensely. Then I was looking out the window, and suddenly James walked by, headed toward one of the project's buildings. I was so excited to see him that I called out to him. I told him to come here for a moment, and he did. I asked him where he was sleeping, and of course I deserved the answer: "None of your business. What does it matter to you? You got what you wanted. You kicked me out of your house and your life. Why are you asking such questions?"

I started apologizing to him and told him I had made a terribly wrong judgment. I asked him, "Can you please come back and let's work it out?" I told him how much I loved him and how much the kids missed him.

He told me he was in the process of handling business, but he left me with this open-ended answer: "If I come later on tonight, we can talk. If you don't see me, I'm not interested anymore." When he walked away, I felt literally in suspense. He had answered me so coldly, but that was to be expected after the way we parted. When I first met him, he was so humble towards me, and I feel as though I had opened a dark side of him that he'd been trying to heal from when I first met him.

All at once I wished I could start over from the day he said he was leaving North Carolina. I wished I had greeted him by meeting him downtown as I'd promised. I felt like a failure in relationships. So I pulled myself together. My friend was coming by to visit me and do my hair, so I showered, got dressed, and waited for her. When she arrived, I started telling her about James. She said she had just seen him up the street by the mailbox. I said I hoped he would come back, but her seeing him still around the neighborhood was a good sign for me that he would return so we could talk.

No sooner had my company left than a knock came at the door. It was James, and he came in. I hugged him, and though I didn't feel one in return, I was okay with that.

He had a right to feel unsure about me. We talked, and he told me he had moved back to New York and was living with one of his relatives. I invited him to come back home, and it didn't take him too long to decide yes. He forgave me, and we prayed for a better next day.

11

The Next Day

*The steadfast love of the Lord never
ceases; his mercies never come to an
end; they are new every morning;
great is your faithfulness.*
—Lamentations 3:22–23

ONE MONDAY MORNING, THE KIDS, JAMES, AND I WERE GETTING
ready for the day. James and I walked the kids up to day
care where they would be until four, so he and I had all
day to be together. We would walk and talk about life and
how we wanted our future to be. We also talked about
how many kids we wanted to have together, but we never

mentioned getting married. So as time went on, in the evening when the kids were home from day care, I was always in the kitchen baking chicken for dinner. James loved the crispy taste of it, so I made chicken often.

Nighttime, after the kids were in bed, James and I often stayed up talking, many times greeting the dawn. He would read the Bible, and I would be dozing in and out, sleeping while he would read. Sometimes I listened, and sometimes not, but one thing I can say is that we both were trying to find God the best way we knew how without guidance.

As time went on, the dark side of James began to show more and more. My kids' father was back around, in and out of their lives, but in reality trying to provoke my relationship with deception. The more that happened, the meaner James got, and the light I was attracted to started to become darker than when we met.

One day my kids' father knocked on our door, wanting James to take a ride with him so they could talk. James had the impression it was the two of them getting together to talk man to man on how to handle his visitation with his children, but instead the ride was to upset James by having a confrontational conversation once again to interrupt our relationship. The way their conversation went was about me still having contact with him to discuss differences James and I had with one another. He said I would tell him about our ups and downs.

On that ride the darker side of James showed up because he didn't accept that information very well. He told my kids' father he knew nothing about him and that he should let him out of the car right away before things got bad. My kids' father didn't know James was going to react like that, so out of fear he let him out and apologized for the misunderstanding. He promised James he wouldn't ever come around again, saying that from now on if he wanted his kids, he would go through a relative for the contact.

James yelled back, letting him know that was how it should've been from the moment he stepped into my life. My kids' father drove off quickly, burning rubber to leave the scene. James took a while to come back home. I started panicking and getting nervous. Hours went by, and finally James popped up, looking very angry. I asked him how did his ride and talk go, and he went off on me. He went on and on, raising his voice, about how I had a nerve to be telling my ex how he and I were having differences with one another as if I still wanted my kids' father.

My heart instantly dropped. How could I have been deceived again? I hadn't considered that a simple conversation from parent to parent could turn out to be an allegation against me once again. James suggested he needed space and that he would look for a rooming house to rent a room. He said he was trying to find the Lord, and he must move quickly before he regretted ever meeting me.

James found a Baptist church and started attending every time the church had a service. I noticed one day he came home with a haircut, and I thought he had another woman that he was seeing, not knowing he was cleaning himself up to be baptized in the Holy Spirit. He would come home and sleep in the living room. Our conversations weren't the same.

Then one day, I woke up to a pastor in my home talking with James in the living room about shacking up and how it was wrong and how it wouldn't work without the Lord, and me not being his wife. He told James he owned a rooming house where James can rent a room as long as he attended church services and had a steady job. James took the offer and left my home to find out if that was truly God's direction and his plan for us to be together and not a lie. God was on the move, and I didn't even see it happening.

12

God Is Moving

So God has given both his promise and his
oath. These two things are unchangeable
because it is impossible for God to lie.
Therefore, we who have fled to him for
refuge can have great confidence as we
hold to the hope that lies before us.
—Hebrews 6:18

MONTHS WENT BY, AND JAMES AND I HAD NOT BEEN LIVING
together, yet he came over from time to time. I thanked
God I was still his girlfriend after all we had been through.

When he came over, the kids and I were happy, never wanting him to leave.

He was changing, but in a good way. When he visited, he invited me to attend his baptism. I accepted, asking myself why he wanted to do that. The fun we used to have, we wouldn't be able to have anymore. Being in love with him, I supported his decision. One day before the baptism, I asked my sister if she would accompany me, and she said yes.

On Sunday I was nervous as a sinner singing in the choir, but I made it to service to witness my boyfriend getting baptized by water, accepting Jesus as his Lord and Savior. I was teary-eyed with joy, witnessing such a beautiful service. When the baptism was over, the pastor did an altar call, and I was drawn by the Holy Spirit, so I went up to get baptized and saved like James for the next Sunday service.

After service, James went back to his home, and I went to mine, waiting to be baptized. Next week came, and I got baptized, thinking that I was going to bring James home with me for good. But James told me. "Jesus doesn't work like that." He said that was the whole reason he was homeless in the first place. God had stripped him so that he could know who God really is for himself. He said I would have to experience the same feeling he did to know God for myself.

Time passed, and I started going back to my old ways but worse than ever before. I was getting messed up every night, drinking from sunup to sun down, having company out of this world, and I didn't care. When you do good, evil is there watching you, laughing at you, and encouraging you to do all the wrong things.

Finally, one night I partied so hard with friends that the next morning one of the guys who'd enjoyed my company partying was still in my apartment. I looked him in the face and yelled, "Out! This is it! I'm going across town to bring my man home. I can't live like this anymore." He walked with me to the day care to pick up my boys and rode with me in a cab across town; he didn't mind the ride because he lived a block over from James.

When I got to James's house, I humbly pleaded with him to come home to me. I told him I couldn't stand the fact that we were not living together and about how much I had changed from being indecisive. I shared with him how my kids' father had gotten saved, gotten married, and moved to another state with his wife to start a new way of living. I also told James that my kids' father and I had agreed to have visitations through the court system.

That evening James was convinced. He saw something different in me. He saw that finally I could be looked at as a woman of my word. He came back to my house but with terms and conditions of his own. He told me how he was tired of being shaken together and how he wanted to get married if we expected God to ever bless our relationship. So he proposed, and I said yes with no hesitation.

James wanted to get married as soon as possible with no wedding and promised me that after some years of marriage, we could renew our vows. At that time I could plan my dream wedding. So he bought the rings, and we eloped. We got married two days after Christmas, and my family members couldn't believe I was married, but they were happy we had tied the knot.

13

Tied the Knot

The man who finds a wife finds a treasure,
and he receives favor from the Lord.
—Proverbs 18:22

ON DECEMBER 27, 2004, I WAS NO LONGER A WINSTON. I became Natasha Ann Scott. I was happily married to the man I fell in love with. The moment we honored God with our vows of marriage was when our blessings began has Mr. and Mrs. We didn't have a chance to have a honeymoon, but we had the chance to go home and plan our future. We both felt different, but it was an awesome feeling to be married.

The next day I called all my close family members to share the good news. Some were happy, and some showed unhappiness. If I was happy, I didn't care about the unhappy people. "This man is a good man, and I went with my spirit."

After a few weeks of living in the projects, I received a letter in the mail asking me if I was still interested in the HUD houses that were new, and we accepted the offer. Newlyweds, new house, and a new beginning. I mailed the acceptance letter back, and in a few weeks, I received another letter to tour the house. My husband, kids, and I were so excited about this move that our decision was already made to sign the lease. Unfortunately we had to follow proper protocol. After we toured the house, they were going to contact us to sign the lease in a few days. The few days we had to wait felt like months because we were so excited. My husband said to throw out everything, and he would buy all new furniture. I couldn't believe the expression of love my husband was showing me, spoiling me the moment I became his wife.

A few days later, we received the call that our keys and lease were ready. This would be our fresh start as living as the Scott Family

14

The Scott Family

How wonderful and pleasant it is when
brothers live together in harmony!
—Psalm 133:1

It was the first day of moving from the projects to our first house as the Scott family. Truly indeed, the Lord was blessing our marriage and our children; truly indeed the Lord was pleased with our decision to become husband and wife, which was pleasing in his sight. My husband had movers in place, and new furniture was arriving. True to his word, he furnished every room in the house. I had the honor of shopping for house accessories. I was in heaven with no care in the world. In the backyard, we had a deck and a huge space for the boys to play in without me having to worry about their safety. God is good. Company started to come over, showering us with housewarming gifts. It was a wonderful feeling of love around us.

Things were going well in our marriage. We had found a new church and were attending every Sunday. My husband joined the choir, and I became an usher. God was on the move. We still had sinful ways, but only God can judge, deliver, and heal. The neighborhood was family oriented, and the neighbors greeted us with love. Our life was headed in the right direction.

My husband obtained his driver's license, and one of the church members gave him a car. He went to training classes to receive his gun permit so he could get a better job for his family. He was hired as an armored truck driver, I got a job as a teacher's assistant working with children in a day care, and the kids were attending an elementary school in walking distance from our home. God was moving in the Scotts' life.

Then on Halloween night, the boys were getting dressed in their power ranger costumes, and I was feeling horrible. I was showing symptoms of a stomach virus, but that stomach virus turned out to be a pregnancy. I couldn't believe the news from the Clearblue test, so I bought a First Response test, which confirmed that I was pregnant.

When my husband called the house as he did every night to check on his family, I told him that I was pregnant. He was excited because this would be his first child. He came home that night very emotional about the news and hugged me tight, saying, "I'm going to be a father. I know I'm already a father to the boys, but I'm blessed by God to have a blood born." Knowing this man the way I knew him now, I wasn't offended at all about what he said. In fact I understood very well. He was an only child, and his mother, his grandmother, and his grandfather all had passed away and left him alone. So having his blood child was a great deal and a blessing.

As time went on, we found out we were having a baby girl due to come into this world in July of 2007.

Soon the baby was here, and she was growing up, and time was passing us by. We found out from the housing manager of HUD that we could no longer stay in the house because we had two boys and a girl living in a two-bedroom, so we had to move. We needed extra space.

Back in 2000, before I met my husband, I had applied for housing in another town, and miraculously, when I called to check the status of my application, the lady told me my name was next on the list. So my husband and I went down to see about the place, and we were told they had a four-bedroom unit. It was a blessing to know we got the place because my husband was working in the same town as the housing development; otherwise, we wouldn't have qualified to live in that town. But God, of course, had a plan. Remember, this was a new walk, and we didn't see where God was taking us, but we trusted that wherever he took us would be for the best. God is good!

The new town was a step up from what we were used to. The school system was different and more structured, which was a plus. A few days later we received a call that the unit was available. God was moving us again. I was excited to be moving to a place with more bedrooms and more space. My husband was happy because he would be living about five minutes from his job.

A week before we were to move, my husband was working part-time at a club as a bouncer. A patron came into the club with a cocky attitude toward my husband. Words were exchanged, and this guy didn't like my husband's reaction and the way he escorted him out of the club because of his rowdiness, disorderly behavior, and roughness. Clearly the guy was under the influence, and he threatened my husband by telling him that he would be waiting for him after club hours.

After the club closed, my husband saw that the guy was waiting for him. My husband got into his car to come home and soon noticed the guy following him. The guy took a shot at my husband's car, and my husband fled down the street. He was driving so fast that he flipped the car. He got out running, and the guy took a shot at him again. This time the bullet hit him, but he didn't notice until some lady saw that he was bleeding from his side. He told her to call 911, and she did. Cops arrived on the scene along with the ambulance, they transferred my husband to the hospital. When he arrived at the hospital, he was told how blessed he was, because there were two holes in him with no wound channel. They said to him that the man upstairs must love him, and my husband looked toward the ceiling and said, "Thank you, God, for showing me your miracles."

Earlier James had called me to say he would be home soon. Many hours later, I heard a knock at the door, and when I opened it, I knew right away something had happened. It was his supervisor from his part-time job, and he stood there holding a bag of my husband's bloody clothes. He said to me immediately, "Don't be alarmed." Of course, I was alarmed to hear that and started praying immediately. He said, "Your husband's been shot, but he'll be fine." He was going to bring him home once the cops did a report on him.

Thank God he was going to be all right. Still, at this point I wanted him home right away. Our car was now a total loss, but I thanked God he was still alive. I'd prefer to be getting a rental car rather than making funeral arrangements.

The next day my husband came home, and I was taking care of his wound. He was able to work, and he was able to still move us to our new apartment all by himself. God had his angels of protection around him and the family. When things are going good, evil is not too far behind, but thank God Jesus had his hedge around us. In the same week all these things were going on, God's plan would still prevail.

15

God's Plan

*And the father who knows all hearts knows
what the Spirit is saying, for the Spirit
pleads for us believers in harmony with
God's own will. And we know that God
causes everything to work together for
the good of those who love God and are
called according to his purpose for them.*
—Romans 8:27–28

IT WAS GOD'S PLAN FOR US TO MOVE TO A NEW LOCATION BECAUSE
for one thing the family was starting to grow. Soon we
were all moved into our new four-bedroom apartment full

of space. The boys were happy to finally have their own bedroom. Having my husband's job only five minutes away was truly a blessing.

We moved in on a weekend, I had time to get ready for Monday to enroll the boys into their new school. At the time I was not working because of the baby. My husband did it all with the strength and the help of the Lord. I was there to help meet the needs in the home. It worked out because we were all in one accord.

We were not attending church services anymore because of differences that had led us to realize we needed more than just singing and reading and being an usher. We would watch services on TV, pray together, and have our own Bible study, but something was still missing—the power we needed to live right in God's sight. Neither one of us had yet obtained it; we both were up and down in our Christianity, still wanting to be partly of the world and partly saved.

Then one day my mother's husband called James and me over to his house to have church. We were attending church at my mother's home for about six months until God called my mother's husband to open a church. The church we worshipped in is an Apostolic Faith church, where we believe in the Holy Ghost and calling on the name of Jesus. That name calling filled my husband up with the Holy Ghost, and Jesus started really working on him. He was called into the ministry in 2009 as an assistant pastor of the church; he is the pastor's right-hand man. I was still battling. During that time, God was still blessing our marriage and blessing my womb plentifully. I became pregnant again with another baby girl, and thirteen months later I had another baby, this time a boy. When our son was born, he was named after his father.

When our son was four months old, I experienced heart failure. We can get only so far off our knees until God finds a way to put us back down. It was a Sunday afternoon. I was experiencing rapid breathing and heart palpitations. James looked at me and said, "You don't look good. I'm calling 911."

I didn't know my blood pressure was sky-high until the paramedics measured it and whispered to my husband, "She's going into congestive heart failure." All I could think of was calling the name of Jesus in my spirit. As they were putting the oxygen on me, I thought I was going to die. Lord knows I never intended to make the Lord this angry. I surely didn't want to leave without fulfilling my calling.

At that moment I repented, and God added more years to my life. Knowing that I didn't dare play with my salvation, I started serving God strongly after I was bought out of the hospital. Four years later I had another baby, another girl, and God said to me, "You are not serving me wholeheartedly." Isn't that like so many of us, pleading with God to save us from a situation, and we go right back after he does? But don't play with God. My body was touched with a blood disorder called thrombocytosis. My bone marrow was tested, and my electrolytes were disordered, and my potassium level was extremely low. Satan wanted my soul to be his, but I didn't go down without a fight, and with God's mercy he brought me out again.

My husband and I prayed together always, but one day I looked at him, and we called on Jesus until I received his Holy Spirit. My husband was always there for me when I was in the Lord and away from the Lord. He never judged me, he always lived up to the standard set by the Bible:

The believing wife brings holiness to her marriage, and the believing husband brings holiness to his marriage. Otherwise your children would not be holy, but now they are holy. (1 Corinthians 7:14)

My husband would say, "You can leave the Lord, but he will never leave you." He also said, "The devil knows your weakness; the devil knows when you're not serious." He told me that the moment I became more serious with my salvation, I would be able to take tests and attacks with more strength.

When covid took over the land and the churches were closed, it forced us all to find the true church. Jesus said, in Luke 17:21, "You won't be able to say, 'Here it is!' or 'It's over there!' For the Kingdom of God is already among you." I found out through ups and downs during the separation from my church family that I was forced to face my tests with no other support except seeking the Spirit of God.

Through it all I feel more confidence as a believer because I've gotten to know God for myself. And who is God? I have come to know he is a healer, a deliverer, a counselor, a friend who sticks closer than a brother, and he is truly a comforter. Finally he is the Holy Ghost, the indwelling power that keeps you from yielding to sin and walking by faith and not by sight (it pays off).

Empowering Scriptures

Here are some encouraging scriptures of faith that help me through storms, and obstacles. These scriptures encouraged me to walk by faith and not by sight. I hope and pray that these inspired scriptures touch your inner soul. I encourage all my readers to get a personal relationship with Christ. If you already have that relationship, keep it. God bless!

> Faith shows the reality of what we hope for;
> it is the evidence of things we cannot see.
> (Hebrews 11:1)

> For we live by believing and not by seeing.
> (2 Corinthians 5:7)

I pray that God, the source of hope, will fill you completely with joy and peace because you trust in him. Then you will overflow with confident hope through the power of the Holy Spirit. (Romans 15:13)

But when you ask him, be sure that your faith is in God alone. Do not waver, for a person with divided loyalty is as unsettled as a wave of the sea that is blown and tossed by the wind. (James 1:6)

And it is impossible to please God without faith. Anyone who wants to come to him must believe that God exists and that he rewards those who sincerely seek him. (Hebrews 11:6)

You love him even though you have never seen him. Though you do not see him now, you trust him; and you rejoice with a glorious, inexpressible joy. The reward for trusting him will be the salvation of your souls. (1 Peter 1:8–9)

Jesus told her, "I am the resurrection and the life. Anyone who believes in me will live, even after dying. Everyone who lives in me and believes in me will never ever die. Do you believe this, Martha?" (John 11:25–26)

You can pray for anything, and if you have faith, you will receive it. (Matthew 21:22)

"You don't have enough faith, "Jesus told them. "I tell you the truth, if you had faith even as small as a mustard seed, you could say to this mountain, move from here to there, and it would move. Nothing would be impossible." (Matthew 17:20)

"Dear woman, "Jesus said to her, "Your faith is great. Your request is granted. "And her daughter was instantly healed. (Matthew 15:28)

For it is by believing in your heart that you are made right with God, and it is by openly declaring your faith that you are saved. (Romans 10:10)

For this is how God loved the world: He gave his one and only Son, so that everyone who believes in him will not perish but have eternal life. (John 3:16)

That is why I said that you will die in your sins; for unless you believe that I am who I am I claim to be, you will die in your sins. (John 8:24)

Be still and know that I am God! I will be honored to every nation. I will be honored throughout the world. (Psalm 46:10)

Testimony

And they have defeated him by the blood
of the Lamb and by their testimony.
And they did not love their lives so
much that they were afraid to die.
—Revelation 12:11

AS A BELIEVER IN CHRIST IT IS MY DUTY TO TALK ABOUT THE
greatness of God, what he has done in my life then, and
what he is doing in my life now. With such great honor
I must give thanks and praise to God for how he took
me on a journey walking by faith, not knowing how the
outcome was going to bring me to meet him and to know
who he is. If my readers have reached this point to hear

my testimony, you are about to hear how I'm going to brag on God.

Walking by faith and not by sight is more than just a book title; it is my personal divine experience through miracles, mercy, grace, and ultimately freedom from sin. I learned that getting out of our eyesight is walking into God's vision and plans for our lives.

I also came to realize that faith doesn't come easy. It's harder to believe something is coming when you have no visual signs, only trusting in God that he has already provided the way. We would have to keep following his vision and not our own sight. I can also assure you if anyone says walking by faith doesn't hurt, believe me, it has its share of pain. When we become blind to the source of the pain and return our sight to the joy of God's vision, we will soon find out that Jesus Christ will come to our rescue to strengthen us, deliver us, and establish us for his glory.

I thank God for my husband, who is a strong believer in God, and for my six children and my grandchildren. I thank God for how my trip to North Carolina paid off because without meeting my husband, I might have never met Jesus like I was predestined to.

I've met a lot of obstacles and challenges, but when I look over my life, God was there also. Jesus brought me through eight pregnancies. I lost two, but through faith God kept me strong in believing the two aren't here for his reasons and not mine. He brought through depression and through addiction to a variety of things that were not pleasing to God. Thanks to him, I've overcome heart failure and a blood disorder, and he has much more for me as long as I keep the faith, seeking him daily and living by walking in the spirit and not letting my flesh rule my life.

Pray always, and keep first walking by faith and not by what you see. God bless and heal your land. Amen, and thank you, Jesus!